99 POEMS IN TRANSLATION

by Harold Pinter

plays

BETRAYAL
THE BIRTHDAY PARTY
THE CARETAKER
THE COLLECTION and THE LOVER
THE HOMECOMING
THE HOTHOUSE
LANDSCAPE and SILENCE
NO MAN'S LAND
OLD TIMES
ONE FOR THE ROAD
OTHER PLACES
(A Kind of Alaska, Victoria Station, Family Voices)
THE ROOM and THE DUMB WAITER
A SLIGHT ACHE and other plays
MOUNTAIN LANGUAGE
PARTY TIME
MOONLIGHT

PLAYS ONE
(The Birthday Party, The Room, The Dumb Waiter,
A Slight Ache, The Hothouse, A Night Out,
The Black and White, The Examination)

PLAYS TWO
(The Caretaker, The Dwarfs, The Collection, The Lover,
Night School, Trouble in the Works, The Black and White,
Request Stop, Last to Go, Special Offer)

PLAYS THREE
(The Homecoming, Tea Party, The Basement, Landscape,
Silence, Night, That's Your Trouble, That's All, Applicant,
Interview, Dialogue for Three, Tea Party (short story))

PLAYS FOUR
(Old Times, No Man's Land, Betrayal, Monologue,
One for the Road, Family Voices, A Kind of Alaska,
Victoria Station, Mountain Language)

screenplays

THE PROUST SCREENPLAY
THE SERVANT and other screenplays
(The Pumpkin Eater, The Quiller Memorandum, Accident,
The Go-Between)
THE FRENCH LIEUTENANT'S WOMAN and other screenplays
(The Last Tycoon, Langrishe, Go Down)
THE HEAT OF THE DAY
THE COMFORT OF STRANGERS and other screenplays
(Reunion, Turtle Diary, Victory)
THE TRIAL

poetry and prose

COLLECTED POEMS AND PROSE
THE DWARFS (a novel)
100 POEMS BY 100 POETS (an anthology)

99 POEMS

IN TRANSLATION

An Anthology selected by

HAROLD PINTER

ANTHONY ASTBURY

GEOFFREY GODBERT

Grove Press
New York

First published in Great Britain in 1994 by Faber and Faber Limited and Greville Press
First Grove Press edition, October 1994

Printed in the United States of America

FIRST PAPERBACK EDITION

Library of Congress Cataloging-in-Publication Data

99 poems in translation: an anthology / selected by Harold Pinter,
    Anthony Astbury, Geoffrey Godbert.—1st ed.
    Includes index.
    ISBN 0-8021-3489-0 (pbk.)
    1. Poetry—Translations into English. I. Pinter, Harold, 1930–
II. Astbury, Anthony. III. Godbert, Geoffrey.
IV. Title: Ninety-nine poems in translation.
PN6101.A15 1994   808.81—dc20   94-21546

Grove Press
841 Broadway
New York, NY 10003

10 9 8 7 6 5 4 3 2 1

Contents

vii

viii

I am not among those who left our land

I am not among those who left our land
to be torn to pieces by our enemies.
I don't listen to their vulgar flattery,
I will not give them my poems.

But the exile is for ever pitiful to me,
like a prisoner, like a sick man.
Your road is dark, wanderer;
alien corn smells of wormwood.

But here, stupefied by fumes of fire,
wasting the remainder of our youth,
we did not defend ourselves
from a single blow.

We know that history
will vindicate our every hour . . .
There is no one in the world more tearless,
more proud, more simple than us.

Translated by RICHARD MCKANE

Amergin's Charm

I am a stag : *of seven tines,*
I am a flood : *across a plain,*
I am a wind : *on a deep lake,*
I am a tear : *the Sun lets fall,*
I am a hawk : *above the cliff,*
I am a thorn : *beneath the nail,*
I am a wonder : *among flowers,*
I am a wizard : *who but I*
Sets the cool head aflame with smoke?

I am a spear : *that roars for blood,*
I am a salmon : *in a pool,*
I am a lure : *from paradise,*
I am a hill : *where poets walk,*
I am a boar : *ruthless and red,*
I am a breaker : *threatening doom,*
I am a tide : *that drags to death,*
I am an infant : *who but I*
Peeps from the unhewn dolmen arch?

I am the womb : *of every holt,*
I am the blaze : *on every hill,*
I am the queen : *of every hive,*
I am the shield : *for every head,*
I am the tomb : *of every hope.*

Translated by ROBERT GRAVES

Song of the Fallen Deer

At the time of the White Dawn;
　　At the time of the White Dawn,
I arose and went away.
　　At Blue Nightfall I went away.

I ate the thornapple leaves
　　And the leaves made me dizzy.
I drank the thornapple flowers
　　And the drink made me stagger.

The hunter, Bow-Remaining,
　　He overtook and killed me,
Cut and threw my horns away.
　　The hunter, Reed-Remaining,
He overtook and killed me,
　　Cut and threw my feet away.

Now the flies become crazy
　　And they drop with flapping wings.
The drunken butterflies sit
　　With opening and shutting wings.

Translated by FRANK RUSSELL

Drinking

The thirsty earth soaks up the rain,
And drinks and gapes for drink again;
The plants suck in the earth, and are
With constant drinking fresh and fair;
The sea itself (which one would think
Should have but little need of drink)
Drinks ten thousand rivers up,
So filled that they o'erflow the cup.
The busy Sun (and one would guess
By's drunken fiery face no less)
Drinks up the sea, and when he's done,
The Moon and Stars drink up the Sun:
They drink and dance by their own light,
They drink and revel all the night:
Nothing in Nature's sober found,
But an eternal health goes round.
Fill up the bowl, then, fill it high,
Fill all the glasses there, for why
Should every creature drink but I,
Why, man of morals, tell me why?

Translated by ABRAHAM COWLEY

CARLOS DRUMMOND DE ANDRADE
1902–1987

to Rodrigo M. F. de Andrade

Travelling in the Family

In the desert of Itabira
the shadow of my father
took me by the hand.
So much time lost.
But he didn't say anything.
It was neither day nor night.
A sigh? A passing bird?
But he didn't say anything.

We have come a long way.
Here there was a house.
The mountain used to be bigger.
So many heaped-up dead,
and time gnawing the dead.
And in the ruined houses,
cold disdain and damp.
But he didn't say anything.

The street he used to cross
on horseback, at a gallop.
His watch. His clothes.
His legal documents.
His tales of love-affairs.
Opening of tin trunks
and violent memories.
But he didn't say anything.

In the desert of Itabira
things come back to life,
stiflingly, suddenly.
The market of desires
displays its sad treasures;
my urge to run away;
naked women; remorse.
But he didn't say anything.

Stepping on books and letters
we travel in the family.
Marriages; mortgages;
the consumptive cousins;
the mad aunt; my grandmother
betrayed among the slave-girls,
rustling silks in the bedroom.
But he didn't say anything.

What cruel, obscure instinct
moved his pallid hand
subtly pushing us
into the forbidden
time, forbidden places?

I looked in his white eyes.
I cried to him: Speak! My voice
shook in the air a moment,
beat on the stones. The shadow
proceeded slowly on
with that pathetic travelling
across the lost kingdom.
But he didn't say anything.

I saw grief, misunderstanding
and more than one old revolt
dividing us in the dark.
The hand I wouldn't kiss,
the crumb that they denied me,
refusal to ask pardon.
Pride. Terror at night.
But he didn't say anything.

Speak speak speak speak.
I pulled him by his coat
that was turning into clay.
By the hands, by the boots
I caught at his strict shadow
and the shadow released itself
with neither haste nor anger.
But he remained silent.

There were distinct silences
deep within his silence.
There was my deaf grandfather
hearing the painted birds
on the ceiling of the church;
my own lack of friends;
and your lack of kisses;
there were our difficult lives
and a great separation
in the little space of the room.

The narrow space of life
crowds me up against you,
and in this ghostly embrace
it's as if I were being burned
completely, with poignant love.
Only now do we know each other!
Eye-glasses, memories, portraits
flow in the river of blood.
Now the waters won't let me
make out your distant face,
distant by seventy years . . .

I felt that he pardoned me
but he didn't say anything.
The waters cover his moustache,
the family, Itabira, all.

Translated by ELIZABETH BISHOP

INNOKENTY ANNENSKY
1856–1909

Black Spring

A half-holiday for the burial. Of course, they punish
the provincial copper bells for hours;
terribly the nose tilts up like a tallow candle
from the coffin. Does it wish to draw breath
from its torso in a mourning.suit? The last snow
fell sombrely – white, then the roads were bread-crumbed
with pebbles.
Poor winter, honeycombed with debts,
poured to corruption. Now the dumb, black springtime
must look into the chilly eye . . . from under the mould
on the roof-shingles, the liquid oatmeal
of the roads, the green stubble of life
on our faces! High in the splinter elm,
shrill the annual fledglings with their spiky necks.
They say to man that his road is mud,
his luck is rutted – there is nothing
sorrier than the marriage of two deaths.

Translated by ROBERT LOWELL

ANONYMOUS
5TH CENTURY BC

Psalm 137

1 By the waters of Babylon we sat down and wept:
when we remembered thee, O Sion.

2 As for our harps, we hanged them up:
upon the trees that are therein.

3 For they that led us away captive
required of us then a song,
and melody, in our heaviness:
Sing us one of the songs of Sion.

4 How shall we sing the Lord's song:
in a strange land?

5 If I forget thee, O Jerusalem:
let my right hand forget her cunning.

6 If I do not remember thee,
let my tongue cleave to the roof of my mouth:
yea, if I prefer not Jerusalem in my mirth.

7 Remember the children of Edom, O Lord,
in the day of Jerusalem:
how they said, Down with it, down with it,
even to the ground.

8 O daughter of Babylon, wasted with misery:
yea, happy shall he be that rewardeth thee,
as thou hast served us.

9 Blessed shall he be that taketh thy children:
and throweth them against the stones.

Translated by MILES COVERDALE

Song of Songs: 7

1 How beautiful are thy feet with shoes,
O prince's daughter!
the joints of thy thighs are like jewels,
the work of the hands of a cunning workman.

2 Thy navel is like a round goblet,
which wanteth not liquor:
thy belly is like an heap of wheat set about with lilies.

3 Thy two breasts are like two young roes
that are twins.

4 Thy neck is as a tower of ivory;
thine eyes like the fishpools in Heshbon, by the gate of Bath-rabbim:
thy nose is as the tower of Lebanon
which looketh toward Damascus.

5 Thine head upon thee is like Carmel,
and the hair of thine head like purple;
the king is held in the galleries.

6 How fair and how pleasant art thou,
O love, for delights!

7 This thy stature is like to a palm tree,
and thy breasts to clusters of grapes.

8 I said, I will go up to the palm tree,
I will take hold of the boughs thereof:
now also thy breasts shall be as clusters of the vine,
and the smell of thy nose like apples;

9 And the roof of thy mouth like the best wine for my beloved,
that goeth down sweetly,
causing the lips of those that are asleep to speak.

10 I am my beloved's,
and his desire is toward me.

11 Come, my beloved,
let us go forth into the field;
let us lodge in the villages.

12 Let us get up early to the vineyards;
let us see if the vine flourish,
whether the tender grape appear,
and the pomegranates bud forth:
there will I give thee my loves.

13 The mandrakes give a smell,
and at our gates are all manner of pleasant fruits,
new and old,
which I have laid up for thee,
O my beloved.

Translators: ANONYMOUS

ANONYMOUS
600–1200

The King of Connacht

'Have you seen Hugh,
The Connacht king in the field?'
'All that we saw
Was his shadow under his shield.'

Translated by FRANK O'CONNOR

Piddle-paddling race of critics, rhizome-fanciers

Piddle-paddling race of critics, rhizome-fanciers
   digging up others' poetry, pusillanimous bookworms
coughing through brambles, aristophobes and Erinnaphils,
   dusty bitter barkers from Callimachus' kennels,
poet's-bane, nightshade of the neophytes,
   bacilli on singing lips: get off, get down, get lost!

Translated by EDWIN MORGAN

GUILLAUME APOLLINAIRE
1880–1918

The Mirabeau Bridge

Under the Mirabeau Bridge the Seine
Flows and our love
Must I be reminded again
How joy came always after pain

Night comes the hour is rung
The days go I remain

Hands within hands we stand face to face
While underneath
The bridge of our arms passes
The loose wave of our gazing which is endless

Night comes the hour is rung
The days go I remain

Love slips away like this water flowing
Love slips away
How slow life is in its going
And hope is so violent a thing

Night comes the hour is rung
The days go I remain

The days pass the weeks pass and are gone
Neither time that is gone
Nor love ever returns again
Under the Mirabeau Bridge flows the Seine

Night comes the hour is rung
The days go I remain

Translated by W. S. MERWIN

17

LOUIS ARAGON
1897–1982

The Lilacs and the Roses

O months of blossoming, months of transfigurations,
May without a cloud and June stabbed to the heart,
I shall not ever forget the lilacs or the roses
Nor those the Spring has kept folded away apart.

I shall not ever forget the tragic sleight-of-hand,
The cavalcade, the cries, the crowd, the sun,
The lorries loaded with love, the Belgian gifts,
The road humming with bees, the atmosphere that spun,
The feckless triumphing before the battle,
The scarlet blood the scarlet kiss bespoke
And those about to die bolt upright in the turrets
Smothered in lilac by a drunken folk.

I shall not ever forget the flower-gardens of France –
Illuminated scrolls from eras more than spent –
Nor forget the trouble of dusk, the sphinx-like silence,
The roses all along the way we went;
Flowers that gave the lie to the soldiers passing
On wings of fear, a fear importunate as a breeze,
And gave the lie to the lunatic push-bikes and the ironic
Guns and the sorry rig of the refugees.

But what I do not know is why this whirl
Of memories always comes to the same point and drops
At Sainte-Marthe . . . a general . . . a black pattern . . .
A Norman villa where the forest stops;
All is quiet here, the enemy rests in the night
And Paris has surrendered, so we have just heard –

I shall never forget the lilacs nor the roses
Nor those two loves whose loss we have incurred:

Bouquets of the first day, lilacs, Flanders lilacs,
Soft cheeks of shadow rouged by death – and you,
Bouquets of the Retreat, delicate roses, tinted
Like far-off conflagrations: roses of Anjou.

Translated by LOUIS MACNEICE

The Albatross

Often the idle mariners at sea
Catch albatrosses, vast birds of the deep,
Companions which follow lazily
Across the bitter gulfs the gliding ship.

They're scarcely set on deck, these heavenly kings,
Before, clumsy, abashed, and full of shame,
They piteously let their great white wings
Beside them drag, oar-like, and halt and lame.

See this winged traveller, so awkward, weak!
He was so fine: how droll and ugly now!
One sailor sticks a cutty in his beak,
Another limps to mock the bird that flew!

The Poet's like the monarch of the clouds
Who haunts the tempest, scorns the bows and slings;
Exiled on earth amid the shouting crowds,
He cannot walk, for he has giant's wings.

Translated by JOANNA RICHARDSON

Antiquitez de Rome

Thou stranger, which for Rome in Rome here seekest,
And nought of Rome in Rome perceiv'st at all,
These same old walls, old arches, which thou seest,
Old palaces, is that which Rome men call.
    Behold what wreak, what ruin, and what waste,
And how that she, which with her mighty power
Tamed all the world, hath tamed herself at last,
The prey of time, which all things doth devour.
    Rome now of Rome is th'only funeral,
And only Rome of Rome hath victory;
Nor ought save Tyber hastening to his fall
Remains of all: O worlds inconstancy.
    That which is firm doth flit and fall away,
    And that is flitting, doth abide and stay.

Translated by EDMUND SPENSER

BERNART DE VENTADORN
fl. c. 1145–1180

The Lark

When I see the lark a-moving
For joy his wings against the sunlight,
Who forgets himself and lets himself fall
For the sweetness which goes into his heart;
Ai! what great envy comes unto me for him whom I see so
rejoicing!
I marvel that my heart melts not for desiring.
Alas! I thought I knew so much
Of Love, and I know so little of it, for I cannot
Hold myself from loving
Her from whom I shall never have anything toward.
She hath all my heart from me, and she hath from me all my wit
And myself and all that is mine.
And when she took it from me she left me naught
Save desiring and a yearning heart.

Translated by EZRA POUND

ALEKSANDR BLOK
1880–1921

The Vulture

Describing circle after circle
a wheeling vulture scans a field
lying desolate. In her hovel
a mother's wailing to her child:
'Come take my breast, boy, feed on this,
grow, know your place, shoulder the cross.'

Centuries pass, villages flame,
are stunned by war and civil war.
My country, you are still the same,
tragic, beautiful as before.
How long must the mother wail?
How long must the vulture wheel?

22nd March 1916

Translated by JON STALLWORTHY *and* PETER FRANCE

BERTOLT BRECHT
1898–1956

War Has Been Given a Bad Name

I am told that the best people have begun saying
How, from a moral point of view, the Second World War
Fell below the standard of the First. The Wehrmacht
Allegedly deplores the methods by which the SS effected
The extermination of certain peoples. The Ruhr industrialists
Are said to regret the bloody manhunts
Which filled their mines and factories with slave workers. The
                                                            intellectuals
So I heard, condemn industry's demand for slave workers
Likewise their unfair treatment. Even the bishops
Dissociate themselves from this way of waging war; in short the
                                                            feeling
Prevails in every quarter that the Nazis did the Fatherland
A lamentably bad turn, and that war
While in itself natural and necessary, has, thanks to the
Unduly uninhibited and positively inhuman
Way in which it was conducted on this occasion, been
Discredited for some time to come.

Translated by JOHN WILLETT

24

ANDRÉ BRETON
1896–1966

Freedom of Love

My wife with the hair of a wood fire
With the thoughts of heat lightning
With the waist of an hourglass
With the waist of an otter in the teeth of a tiger
My wife with the lips of a cockade and of a bunch of stars of the
last magnitude
With the teeth of tracks of white mice on the white earth
With the tongue of rubbed amber and glass
My wife with the tongue of a stabbed host
With the tongue of a doll that opens and closes its eyes
With the tongue of an unbelievable stone
My wife with the eyelashes of strokes of a child's writing
With brows of the edge of a swallow's nest
My wife with the brow of slates of a hothouse roof
And of steam on the panes
My wife with shoulders of champagne
And of a fountain with dolphin-heads beneath the ice
My wife with wrists of matches
My wife with fingers of luck and ace of hearts
With fingers of mown hay
My wife with armpits of marten and of beechnut
And of Midsummer Night
Of privet and of an angelfish nest
With arms of seafoam and of riverlocks
And of a mingling of the wheat and the mill
My wife with legs of flares
With the movements of clockwork and despair
My wife with calves of eldertree pith

My wife with feet of initials
With feet of rings of keys and Java sparrows drinking
My wife with a neck of unpearled barley
My wife with a throat of the valley of gold
Of a tryst in the very bed of the torrent
With breasts of night
My wife with breasts of a marine molehill
My wife with breasts of the ruby's crucible
With breasts of the rose's spectre beneath the dew
My wife with the belly of an unfolding of the fan of days
With the belly of a gigantic claw
My wife with the back of a bird fleeing vertically
With a back of quicksilver
With a back of light
With a nape of rolled stone and wet chalk
And of the drop of a glass where one has just been drinking
My wife with hips of a skiff
With hips of a chandelier and of arrow-feathers
And of shafts of white peacock plumes
Of an insensible pendulum
My wife with buttocks of sandstone and asbestos
My wife with buttocks of swans' backs
My wife with buttocks of spring
With the sex of an iris
My wife with the sex of a mining-placer and of a platypus
My wife with a sex of seaweed and ancient sweetmeat
My wife with a sex of mirror
My wife with eyes full of tears
With eyes of purple panoply and of a magnetic needle
My wife with savanna eyes

My wife with eyes of water to be drunk in prison
My wife with eyes of wood always under the axe
My wife with eyes of water-level of air earth and fire

Translated by EDOUARD RODITI

ISOBEL CAMPBELL

c. 1200

A Learned Mistress

Tell him it's all a lie;
    I love him as much as my life;
He needn't be jealous of me –
    I love him and loathe his wife.

If he kill me through jealousy now
    His wife will perish of spite,
*He'*ll die of grief for his wife –
    Three of us dead in a night.

All blessings from heaven to earth
    On the head of the woman I hate,
And the man I love as my life,
    Sudden death be his fate.

Translated by FRANK O'CONNOR

Less pub than brothel, and you, the regulars

Less pub than brothel, and you, the regulars
The ninth pillar from Castor and Pollux
Do you think you are the only ones equipped with a penis,
That you are the only ones licensed for fucking
And that the rest who do it are merely goats?
Do you think, as you sit waiting in rows
A hundred or two hundred together, that I shall not dare
To do the whole lot of you, two hundred together?
Think again: I will draw scorpions
All over the walls of the place.
For my girl, who has escaped from my arms,
Who was loved as much, and more than any is loved,
For whom I have expended all my forces,
She is there. You, the great and the good, all love her,
You the valueless, corrupt, adulterous all love her;
You above all Egnatius
Long-haired son of a rabbit-toothed Celtiberian,
Only made good by your beard
Your teeth whitened by Spanish piss.

Translated by C. H. SISSON

The City

You said, 'I will go to another land, I will go to another sea.
Another city will be found, a better one than this.
Every effort of mine is a condemnation of fate;
and my heart is – like a corpse – buried.
How long will my mind remain in this wasteland.
Wherever I turn my eyes, wherever I may look
I see black ruins of my life here,
where I spent so many years destroying and wasting.'

You will find no new lands, you will find no other seas.
The city will follow you. You will roam the same
streets. And you will age in the same neighbourhoods;
and you will grow gray in these same houses.
Always you will arrive in this city. Do not hope for any other –
There is no ship for you, there is no road.
As you have destroyed your life here
in this little corner, you have ruined it in the entire world.

Translated by RAE DALVEN

PAUL CELAN
1920–1970

Deathfugue

Black milk of daybreak we drink it at evening
we drink it at midday and morning we drink it at night
we drink and we drink
we shovel a grave in the air there you won't lie too cramped
A man lives in the house he plays with his vipers he writes
he writes when it grows dark to Deutschland your golden hair
           Marguerite
he writes it and steps out of doors and the stars are all sparkling
         he whistles his hounds to come close
he whistles his Jews into rows has them shovel a grave in the
              ground
he orders us strike up and play for the dance

Black milk of daybreak we drink you at night
we drink you at morning and midday we drink you at evening
we drink and we drink
A man lives in the house he plays with his vipers he writes
he writes when it grows dark to Deutschland your golden hair
           Marguerite
your ashen hair Shulamith we shovel a grave in the sky there you
         won't lie too cramped
He shouts jab the earth deeper you lot there you others sing up
           and play
he grabs for the rod in his belt he swings it his eyes they are blue
jab your spades deeper you lot there you others play on for the
           dancing

31

Black milk of daybreak we drink you at night
we drink you at midday and morning we drink you at evening
we drink and we drink
a man lives in the house your goldenes Haar Marguerite
your aschenes Haar Shulamith he plays with his vipers
He shouts play death more sweetly Death is a master from
                                                    Deutschland
he shouts scrape your strings darker you'll rise then in smoke to
                                                    the sky
you'll have a grave then in the clouds there you won't lie too
                                                    cramped

Black milk of daybreak we drink you at night
we drink you at midday Death is a master aus Deutschland
we drink you at evening and morning we drink and we drink
this Death is ein Meister aus Deutschland his eye it is blue
he shoots you with shot made of lead shoots you level and true
a man lives in the house your goldenes Haar Margarete
he looses his hounds on us grants us a grave in the air
he plays with his vipers and daydreams der Tod ist ein Meister
                                                    aus Deutschland

dein goldenes Haar Margarete
dein aschenes Haar Sulamith

Translated by JOHN FELSTINER

BLAISE CENDRARS
1887–1961

White Suit

I walk on the bridge in my white suit that I bought in Dakar
On my feet my rope sandals bought at Villa Garcia
In my hand my Basque cap brought back from Biarritz
My pockets are full of Caporals Ordinaires
From time to time I sniff my little wooden box from Russia
I jingle the small change in my pocket and a pound sterling in
                                                          gold
I have my big Calabrian handkerchief and these wax matches of
                          a size you don't find anywhere but in London
I am clean washed scrubbed more than the deck
Happy as a king
Rich as a millionaire
Free as a man

Translated by PETER HOIDA

33

DAFYDD AP GWILYM
fl. 1340–1370

The Rattle Bag

As I lay, fullness of praise,
On a summer day under
Trees between field and mountain
Awaiting my soft-voiced girl,
She came, there's no denying,
Where she vowed, a very moon.
Together we sat, fine theme,
The girl and I, debating,
Trading, while I had the right,
Words with the splendid maiden.

And so we were, she was shy,
Learning to love each other,
Concealing sin, winning mead,
An hour lying together,
And then, cold comfort, it came,
A blare, a bloody nuisance,
A sack's bottom's foul seething
From an imp in shepherd's shape,
Who had, public enemy,
A harsh-horned sag-cheeked rattle.
He played, cramped yellow belly,
This bag, curse its scabby leg.
So before satisfaction
The sweet girl panicked: poor me!
When she heard, feeble-hearted,
The stones whir, she would not stay.

By Christ, no Christian country,
Cold harsh tune, has heard the like.
Noisy pouch perched on a pole,
Bell of pebbles and gravel,
Saxon rocks making music
Quaking in a bullock's skin,
Crib of three thousand beetles,
Commotion's cauldron, black bag,
Field-keeper, comrade of straw,
Black-skinned, pregnant with splinters,
Noise that's an old buck's loathing,
Devil's bell, stake in its crotch,
Scarred pebble-bearing belly,
May it be sliced into thongs.
May the churl be struck frigid,
Amen, who scared off my girl.

Translated by JOSEPH CLANCY

Sonnet: Dante Alighieri to Guido Cavalcanti

Guido, I would that Lapo, thou, and I,
Led by some strong enchantment, might ascend
A magic ship, whose charmèd sails should fly
With winds at will where'er our thoughts might wend,
So that no change, nor any evil chance
Should mar our joyous voyage; but it might be,
That even satiety should still enhance
Between our hearts their strict community:
And that the bounteous wizard then would place
Vanna and Bice and my gentle love,
Companions of our wandering, and would grace
With passionate talk, wherever we might rove,
Our time, and each were as content and free
As I believe that thou and I should be.

Translated by PERCY BYSSHE SHELLEY

PAUL ÉLUARD
1895–1952

The Invention

The right hand winnows the sand
Every transformation is possible.

After the stones the sun whets his fever to have done
The description of the landscape is not very important
The pleasant space of harvesting and no longer

Clear with my two eyes
As water and fire.

What is the role of the root?
Despair has broken all his bonds
He carries his hands to his head
One seven one four one two one one
A hundred women in the street
Whom I shall never see again.

The art of living, liberal art, the art of dying well, the art of
thinking, incoherent art, the art of smoking, the art of
enjoying, the art of the Middle Ages, decorative art, the art of
reasoning, the art of reasoning well, poetic art, mechanic art,
erotic art, the art of being a grandfather, the art of the dance,
the art of seeing, the art of being accomplished, the art of
caressing, Japanese art, the art of playing, the art of eating,
the art of torturing.

Yet I have never found what I write in what I love.

Translated by SAMUEL BECKETT

The Measures Taken

The lazy are slaughtered
the world grows industrious

The ugly are slaughtered
the world grows beautiful

The foolish are slaughtered
the world grows wise

The sick are slaughtered
the world grows healthy

The sad are slaughtered
the world grows merry

The old are slaughtered
the world grows young

The enemies are slaughtered
the world grows friendly

The wicked are slaughtered
the world grows good

Translated by MICHAEL HAMBURGER

The Prison

The earth is a prison to man all his life.
Therefore I say this truth to the fool:
though you rush about, the sky
surrounds you on all sides. Try to get
out, if you can.

Translated by T. CARMI

HEINRICH HEINE
1797–1856

Looking Back

I have smelled all the perceptible smells
In this world's kitchen. All things enjoyable
I have enjoyed if ever a man did. I have
Drunk coffee, eaten cake, had a variety
Of fair females, have worn silk waistcoats,
Worn the most elegant tails, and have jingled
A shilling or two in my pocket. I have
Ridden on a high horse like Jonathan Swift.
I owned a house; I also owned a castle.
I reclined on the green fields of good fortune,
And the sun's gold glance wished me good morning.
A laurel wreath moreover I wore; it subtly
Suffused my brain with dreams. I dreamed,
Dreamed of roses, and of eternal spring –
It was all so delicious as long as it lasted:
Dozing in twilight, bone idle, the pigeons,
Yes, roast pigeons literally flew into my mouth,
And angels visited me, producing bottles of
Champagne from their pockets – these were the visions,
Soap bubbles, which burst. The grass I now lie on
Is wet, I am crippled with rheumatism,
And my soul, my very soul is ashamed.
Oh, every joy and every pleasure I paid for
With heartache, sour, I was soaked in bitterness,
Eaten by bugs, by black care oppressed,
Driven to deceit, borrowing cash from
Affluent chaps and doddering harridans –
I believe I was even obliged to go begging.

I'm weary now of all this hither-and-thithering.
I want to sleep it all off in a good deep grave.
So then good-bye! Oh yes, up there good Christian brothers,
Naturally we shall see each other up there again.

Translated by CHRISTOPHER MIDDLETON

A Sad State of Freedom

You waste the attention of your eyes,
the glittering labour of your hands,
and knead the dough enough for dozens of loaves
        of which you'll taste not a morsel;
you are free to slave for others –
you are free to make the rich richer.

The moment you're born
        they plant around you
mills that grind lies
lies to last you a lifetime.
You keep thinking in your great freedom
        a finger on your temple
                free to have a free conscience.

Your head bent as if half-cut from the nape,
your arms long, hanging,
you saunter about in your great freedom:
        you're free
                with the freedom of being unemployed.

You love your country
as the nearest, most precious thing to you.
But one day, for example,
        they may endorse it over to America,
and you, too, with your great freedom –
you have the freedom to become an air-base.

The tentacles of Wall Street may grab you by the neck;
they could despatch you to Korea
        one of these days
there to fill a hollow with your Great Freedom.
Yes, you're free
        with the freedom of an unknown soldier.

You may proclaim that one must live
not as a tool, a number or a link
but as a human being —
then at once they handcuff your wrists.
You are free to be arrested, imprisoned
        and even hanged.

There's neither an iron, wooden
        nor a tulle curtain
          in your life;
there's no need to choose freedom:
you are free.
But this kind of freedom
        is a sad affair under the stars.

Translated by TANER BAYBARS

Tibullus, pull yourself together!

Tibullus, pull yourself together!
You mustn't make such heavy weather
    When women throw you over.
All day you melt in songs of woe,
Merely because a younger beau
    Is now Neaera's lover.

The slender-brow'd Lycoris burns
For Cyrus: presto, Cyrus turns
    To court the peevish Julia;
But Julia will no more abate
Her virgin pride, than does will mate
    With wolves from wild Apulia.

Thus Venus plays her grimmest joke;
She loves to match beneath her yoke
    Those who have least in common,
And both in looks and characters
Concocts the most unlikely pairs –
    No help for man or woman!

Take my own case: I might have wooed
A girl as fair as she was good,
    And here you see me slaving,
In utter bliss, for Myrtale,
A slut, more tetchy than the sea
    Round southern headlands raving.

Translated by EDWARD MARSH

JACOPONE DA TODI
1228–1306

The Stabat Mater

The sorrowing mother was
standing beside the cross
    her son died on
as through her heart of hearts
pain like a flock of darts
    flew sobbing in.

O such affliction then
the mother of this son
    knew as she saw him,
she trembled where she stood
felt her own flesh and blood
    rush to adore him.

Who is the one will not
weep to see all that
    this woman suffers?
who without compassion
look on the immolation
    that she offers?

She saw her son rejected
her own son whipped and tortured
    for all men;
she saw him hang in torment
till at the holy moment
    he lived again.

Fountainhead of sorrow
O mother teach me also
    to love as I mourn,
tender me so much of
your sorrow and your love
    that my tears burn.

And, mother, grant that I
may seem also to die
    on my own cross
and let me also share
those wounds I cannot bear
    since they are his.

I gather my grief with
the tearglass of the truth
    and hope I may give
for that man crucified
tears not to be dried
    as long as I live.

Virgin of virgins, be
turned not away from me:
    grant I may bear
his death within me so
that I may also know
    how to die here.

Burning and burning, by
you, virgin mother, I
    beg to be sheltered
when at the Day of Wrath
by that tremendous death
    everything's altered.

Virgin and queen of virgins
when that last day begins
    O let me see
the dawn break on his face
and let his breath like peace
    be borne upon me.

Grant me the shadowing
hand of his harrowing
    nailed out on wood
and fortified underneath
the crosstree of his death
    stand where you stood.

And when the flesh is dead
heaven from overhead
    send down to me
out of the holy skies
the bird of paradise
    from you to me.

Translated by GEORGE BARKER

Green

Green was the maiden, green, green!
Green her eyes were, green her hair.

The wild rose in her green wood
was neither red nor white, but green.

Through the green air she came.
(The whole earth turned green for her.)

The shining gauze of her garment
was neither blue nor white, but green.

Over the green sea she came.
(And even the sky turned green then.)

My life will always leave unlatched
a small green gate to let her in.

Translated by J. B. TREND *and* J. L. GILI

PIERRE JEAN JOUVE
1887–1976

We have amazed by our great sufferings

We have amazed by our great sufferings
. The inclination of the indifferent stars
We have stared at the blood of the wound
With an outsider's eye, in secret we
Have coupled through the false back door,

We have become these iron systems
Which wander distanceless, caterpillar horsemen
Of the last judgement, a vast, dismal boredom
Bears us to your hoofs of consummation
Red Horse black Horse yellow Horse white Horse.

Translated by KEITH BOSLEY

The Seventh

If you set out in this world,
better be born seven times.
Once, in a house on fire,
once, in a freezing flood,
once, in a wild madhouse,
once, in a field of ripe wheat,
once, in an empty cloister,
and once among pigs in a sty.
Six babes crying, not enough:
you yourself must be the seventh.

When you must fight to survive,
let your enemy see seven.
One, away from work on Sunday,
one, starting his work on Monday,
one, who teaches without payment,
one, who learned to swim by drowning,
one, who is the seed of a forest,
and one, whom wild forefathers protect,
but all their tricks are not enough:
you yourself must be the seventh.

If you want to find a woman,
let seven men go for her.
One, who gives his heart for words,
one, who takes care of himself,
one, who claims to be a dreamer,
one, who through her skirt can feel her,
one, who knows the hooks and snaps,

one, who steps upon her scarf:
let them buzz like flies around her.
You yourself must be the seventh.

If you write and can afford it,
let seven men write your poem.
One, who builds a marble village,
one, who was born in his sleep,
one, who charts the sky and knows it,
one, whom words call by his name,
one, who perfected his soul,
one, who dissects living rats.
Two are brave and four are wise;
you yourself must be the seventh.

And if all went as was written,
you will die for seven men.
One, who is rocked and suckled,
one, who grabs a hard young breast,
one, who throws down empty dishes,
one, who helps the poor to win,
one, who works till he goes to pieces,
one, who just stares at the moon.
The world will be your tombstone:
you yourself must be the seventh.

Translated by JOHN BATKI

This coloured counterfeit that thou beholdest

This coloured counterfeit that thou beholdest,
vainglorious with the excellencies of art,
is, in fallacious syllogisms of colour,
nought but a cunning dupery of sense;

this in which flattery has undertaken
to extenuate the hideousness of years,
and, vanquishing the outrages of time,
to triumph o'er oblivion and old age,

is an empty artifice of care,
is a fragile flower in the wind,
is a paltry sanctuary from fate,
is a foolish sorry labour lost,
is conquest doomed to perish and, well taken,
is corpse and dust, shadow and nothingness.

Translated by SAMUEL BECKETT

A Secret Kept

The girl brought me into the house of love.
She was as pure and perfect as Abigail.
When she took off her veil she revealed a form
That put to shame the beauty of Esther.
Her light shone in the darkness, made everything tremble.
The hills started to dance like rams.
I thought; 'Now our secrets are discovered.'
But she stretched out her hand like a woman of strength
And enveloped me with her jet-black hair.
So the day was immediately turned into night.

Translated by DAVID GOLDSTEIN

Opposition

In my youth
I was opposed to school.
And now, again,
I'm opposed to work.

Above all it is health
And righteousness that I hate the most.
There's nothing so cruel to man
As health and honesty.

Of course I'm opposed to 'the Japanese spirit'
And duty and human feeling make me vomit.
I'm against any government anywhere
And show my bum to authors' and artists' circles.

When I'm asked for what I was born,
Without scruple, I'll reply, 'To oppose.'
When I'm in the east
I want to go to the west.

I fasten my coat at the left, my shoes right and left.
My hakama I wear back to front and I ride a horse facing its
                                                    buttocks.

What everyone else hates I like
And my greatest hate of all is people feeling the same.

This I believe: to oppose
Is the only fine thing in life.
To oppose is to live.
To oppose is to get a grip on the very self.

Translated by GEOFFREY BOWNAS *and* ANTHONY THWAITE

VELIMIR KHLEBNIKOV
1885–1922

We chant and enchant

We chant and enchant,
Oh charming enchantment!
No raving, no ranting,
No canting enchantment!
This ranting enchantress
Has cast her enchantment –
We see what her chant meant!
Here rant! There cant!
You charming enchanter,
Cast out her enchantment,
Uncast it, uncant it,
Discast it, discant it,
Descant: Decant! Recant!
He can't. She can't.
Why can't she recant?
Why can't he uncant?
Ranting chanting,
No recanting.
Discant, descant.

Translated by PAUL SCHMIDT

No

It's not because I'm now too old,
More wizened than you guess . . .

If I say no, it's only
Because I fear that yes
Would bring me nothing, in the end,
But a fiercer loneliness.

Translated by GRAEME WILSON

For the Book of Love

I can die tomorrow and I have not loved.
My lips never touched a woman's while I lived.
None has given me her soul in a look; none in heat
Has held me, exhausted with love, to her heart.

I have but suffered for all nature, each moment,
For the beings, the wind, the flowers, the firmament,
Suffered through all my nerves minutely, like a knife,
Suffered to have a soul still not yet pure enough.

I spat upon love, and I have killed the flesh.
Mad with pride on this Earth enslaved by Instinct's leash,
I alone stood and stiffened myself against life.
I challenged the Instinct with a bitter laugh.

Everywhere, in the salons, at the theatre, in church,
Before these cold great men, these men of finest touch,
And these women with gentle, or jealous, or proud eyes
Whose tender, ravished soul one might virginally rechase,

I thought: all these are come to it. I heard in their rites
The roarings of the unclean coupling of brutes.
So much mire with an access of three minutes in mind!
Men, be correct! O women, keep your smiles refined!

Translated by VERNON WATKINS

VALÉRY LARBAUD
1881–1957

Alma Perdida

To you, vague aspirations; enthusiasms;
Thoughts after lunch; emotional impulses;
Feelings that follow the gratification
Of natural needs; flashes of genius; agitation
Of the digestive process; appeasement
Of good digestion; inexplicable joys;
Circulatory problems; memories of love;
Scent of benzoin in the morning tub; dreams of love;
My tremendous Castilian joking, my vast
Puritan sadness, my special tastes:
Chocolate, candies so sweet they almost burn, iced drinks;
Drowsy cigars; you, sleepy cigarettes;
Joys of speed; sweetness of being seated; excellence
Of sleeping in total darkness;
Great poetry of banal things; news items; trips;
Gypsies; sleigh rides; rain on the sea;
Delirium of feverish night, alone with a few books;
Ups and downs of temperature and temperament;
Recurring moments from another life; memories, prophecies;
O splendours of the common life and the usual this and that,
To you this lost soul.

Translated by RON PADGETT *and* BILL ZAVATSKY

To Himself

Now be for ever still,
Weary my heart. For the last cheat is dead,
I thought eternal. Dead. For us, I know
Not only the dear hope
Of being deluded gone, but the desire.
Rest still forever. You
Have beaten long enough. And to no purpose
Were all your stirrings; earth not worth your sighs.
Boredom and bitterness
Is life; and the rest, nothing; the world is dirt.
Lie quiet now. Despair
For the last time. Fate granted to our kind
Only to die. And now you may despise
Yourself, nature, the brute
Power which, hidden, ordains the common doom,
And all the immeasurable emptiness of things.

Translated by JOHN HEATH-STUBBS

The Testament

How much I wanted them to go
And let me be alone with you!
They say I can't last long: I know,
Brother, that what they say is true.

You'll soon be getting leave, no doubt.
Look here – but no; when I pass out
I think there's no one over there
Who'll worry much for that, or care.

So let it be; but if they do
Ask after me – no matter who –
Tell them what happened: you can say
I stopped a bullet yesterday.

Tell them I fought for home and Tsar,
And say what fools the doctors are,
And how to the old country I
Said you must say for me good-bye.

I don't suppose Mother and Dad
Are still alive; but if they were,
What should you say? I wouldn't care,
I must confess, to make them sad.

So, if they're living, he or she,
Just say they mustn't fret for me:
Tell them the regiment's been fighting,
And I was always bad at writing.

There was a girl who lived near-by;
Perhaps she has forgot my name;
So long ago we said good-bye,
She may not ask; but all the same,

Tell her what's happened, plain and bare;
That empty heart you need not spare;
Just let her cry and have her say;
Tears cost her nothing, anyway.

Translated by FRANCES CORNFORD *and* ESTHER POLIANOWSKY SALAMAN

Shemà

You who live secure
In your warm houses,
Who return at evening to find
Hot food and friendly faces:

> Consider whether this is a man,
> Who labours in the mud
> Who knows no peace
> Who fights for a crust of bread
> Who dies at a yes or a no.
> Consider whether this is a woman,
> Without hair or name
> With no more strength to remember
> Eyes empty and womb cold
> As a frog in winter.

Consider that this has been:
I commend these words to you.
Engrave them on your hearts
When you are in your house, when you walk on your way,
When you go to bed, when you rise.
Repeat them to your children.
Or may your house crumble,
Disease render you powerless,
Your offspring avert their faces from you.

Translated by RUTH FELDMAN *and* BRIAN SWANN

The River Merchant's Wife: A Letter

While my hair was still cut straight across my forehead
I played about the front gate, pulling flowers.
You came by on bamboo stilts, playing horse,
You walked about my seat, playing with blue plums.
And we went on living in the village of Chokan:
Two small people, without dislike or suspicion.

At fourteen I married My Lord you.
I never laughed, being bashful.
Lowering my head, I looked at the wall.
Called to, a thousand times, I never looked back.

At fifteen I stopped scowling,
I desired my dust to be mingled with yours
Forever and forever and forever.
Why should I climb the look out?

At sixteen you departed,
You went into far Ku-to-yen, by the river of swirling eddies,
And you have been gone five months.
The monkeys make sorrowful noise overhead.

You dragged your feet when you went out.
By the gate now, the moss is grown, the different mosses,
Too deep to clear them away!
The leaves fall early this autumn, in wind.
The paired butterflies are already yellow with August
Over the grass in the West garden;
They hurt me. I grow older.
If you are coming down through the narrows of the river Kiang,

Please let me know beforehand,
And I will come out to meet you
                    As far as Cho-fu-Sa,

Translated by EZRA POUND

The Faithless Wife

So I took her to the river
believing she was a maiden,
but she already had a husband.

It was on Saint James's night
and almost as if I was obliged to.
The lanterns went out
and the crickets lighted up.
In the farthest street corners
I touched her sleeping breasts,
and they opened to me suddenly
like spikes of hyacinth.
The starch of her petticoat
sounded in my ears
like a piece of silk
rent by ten knives.
Without silver light on their foliage
the trees had grown larger
and a horizon of dogs
barked very far from the river.

Past the blackberries,
the reeds and the hawthorn,
underneath her cluster of hair
I made a hollow in the earth.
I took off my tie.
She took off her dress.
I my belt with the revolver.
She her four bodices.

Nor nard nor mother-o'-pearl
have skin so fine,
nor did crystals lit by moon
shine with such brilliance.
Her thighs slipped away from me
like startled fish,
half full of fire,
half full of cold.
That night I ran
on the best of roads
mounted on a nacre mare
without bridle or stirrups.
As a man, I won't repeat
the things she said to me.
The light of understanding
has made me most discreet.
Smeared with sand and kisses
I took her away from the river.
The swords of the lilies
battled with the air.

I behaved just like myself.
Like a proper gypsy.
I gave her a large sewing basket,
of straw-coloured satin,
and I did not fall in love
for although she had a husband
she told me she was a maiden
when I took her to the river.

Translated by STEPHEN SPENDER *and* J. L. GILI

ANTONIO MACHADO
1875–1939

The Ephemeral Past

Habitué of a small-town club, this man
who saw Carancha poised one day
to take the bull,
has a withered skin, hair going grey,
eyes dim with disenchantment, and beneath
the grey moustache, lips bent
in nausea and a look
that's sad – yet sadness it is not
but something more, and less: the void
of the world in the hollow of his head. He still
sports a jacket coloured currant-red
in a three pile velvet, breeches
booted at their extremities and a caramel
Córdoba hat, turned and furbished well.
Three times he inherited, then lost the lot
three times at cards and twice
was widowed. An illegal round of chance
alone will make him brighten
sprawled at the green baize table;
once more the blood begins to flow
as he recollects a gambler's luck
or the afternoon of some torero,
drinks in an episode from the life
of a daring bandit of the road
or the bloody prowess of a knife.
He satirizes with a yawn the government's
reactionary politics and then
predicts the liberals will come to power

again, just as the stork returns to the bell-tower.
Something of the farmer still, he eyes
the heavens, fears them and at times will sigh
thinking of his olives and, disconsolate,
watches for weather-signs when rain is late.
For the rest, boredom. Taciturn, hypochondriac,
shut in the Arcadia of the present,
and to his brow
only the movement of the smoke gives now
its look of thought. This man is neither
of yesterday nor tomorrow
but of never. Hispanic stock, he's not
the fruit that grew to ripen or to rot,
but shadow-fruit
from a Spain that did not come to be,
that passed away, yet, dead,
persists to haunt us with a greying head.

Translated by CHARLES TOMLINSON *and* HENRY GIFFORD

A lace curtain self-destructs

A lace curtain self-destructs
in its supremely uncertain
fling at exposing only
the shock of a bed's final absence.

The concerted all-white internecine
fight of this hanging thing
dashed against a wan pane
flutters more than it lays to rest.

Under the dreamer's golden canopy, though,
there languishes a lute
with its deep musical emptiness

which turned towards a window
could from its belly alone
give birth to you like a son.

Translated by CHRISTOPHER REID

OSIP MANDELSTAM
1891–1938

The Stalin Epigram

Our lives no longer feel ground under them.
At ten paces you can't hear our words.

But whenever there's a snatch of talk
it turns to the Kremlin mountaineer,

the ten thick worms his fingers,
his words like measures of weight,

the huge laughing cockroaches on his top lip,
the glitter of his boot-rims.

Ringed with a scum of chicken-necked bosses
he toys with the tributes of half-men.

One whistles, another meouws, a third snivels.
He pokes out his finger and he alone goes boom.

He forges decrees in a line like horseshoes,
One for the groin, one the forehead, temple, eye.

He rolls the executions on his tongue like berries.
He wishes he could hug them like big friends from home.

November 1933

Translated by CLARENCE BROWN *and* W. S. MERWIN

Either get out of the house or conform to my tastes, woman

Either get out of the house or conform to my tastes, woman.
I'm no strait-laced old Roman.
I like prolonging the nights agreeably with wine: you, after one
glass of water,
Rise and retire with an air of hauteur.
You prefer darkness: I enjoy love-making
With a witness – a lamp shining or the dawn breaking.
You wear bed-jackets, tunics, thick woollen stuff,
Whereas I think no woman on her back can ever be naked
enough.
I love girls who kiss like doves and hang round my neck:
You give me the sort of peck
Due to your grandmother as a morning salute.
In bed, you're motionless, mute –
Not a wriggle
Not a giggle –
As solemn as a priestess at a shrine
Proffering incense and pure wine.
Yet every time Andromache went for a ride
In Hector's room, the household slaves used to masturbate
outside;
Even modest Penelope, when Ulysses snored,
Kept her hand on the sceptre of her lord.
You refuse to be buggered; but it's a known fact
That Gracchus', Pompey's and Brutus' wives were willing
partners in the act,

And that before Ganymede mixed Jupiter his tasty bowl
Juno filled the dear boy's role.
If you want to be uptight – all right,
By all means play Lucretia by day. But I need a Laïs at night.

Translated by JAMES MICHIE

VLADIMIR MAYAKOVSKY
1893–1930

What About You?

I splintered the landscape of midday
by splashing colours from a tumbler.
I charted on a tray of aspic
the slanting cheekbones of Atlantis.
Upon the scales of an iron turbot,
I found ladies' lips, aloof.
And you,
            could you have played a nocturne
using a drainpipe for a flute?

Translated by MARIA ENZENSBERGER

74

HENRI MICHAUX
1899–1984

Simplicity

What has been particularly lacking in my life up to now is simplicity. Little by little I am beginning to change.

For instance, I always go out with my bed now and when a woman pleases me, I take her and go to bed with her immediately.

If her ears are ugly and large, or her nose, I remove them along with her clothes and put them under the bed, for her to take back when she leaves; I keep only what I like.

If her underthings would improve by being changed, I change them immediately. This is my gift. But if I see a better-looking woman go by, I apologize to the first and make her disappear at once.

People who know me claim that I am incapable of doing what I have just described, that I haven't enough spunk. I once thought so myself, but that was because I was not then doing everything *just as I pleased.*

Now I always have excellent afternoons. (Mornings I work.)

Translated by RICHARD ELLMANN

To Giovanni da Pistoja

On the Painting of the Sistine Chapel

I've grown a goitre by dwelling in this den —
as cats from stagnant streams in Lombardy,
or in what other land they hap to be —
which drives the belly close beneath the chin:

my beard turns up to heaven; my nape falls in,
fixed on my spine: my breast-bone visibly
grows like a harp: a rich embroidery
bedews my face from brush-drops thick and thin.

My loins into my paunch like levers grind:
my buttock like a crupper bears my weight;
my feet unguided wander to and fro;

in front my skin grows loose and long; behind,
by bending it becomes more taut and strait;
crosswise I strain me like a Syrian bow:
    whence false and quaint, I know,
must be the fruit of squinting brain and eye;
for ill can aim the gun that bends awry.
    Come then, Giovanni, try
to succour my dead pictures and my fame;
since foul I fare and painting is my shame.

Translated by JOHN ADDINGTON SYMONDS

Strophes

It will be as it is in this life, the same room,
Yes, the same! and at daybreak, the bird of time in the leafage,
Pale as a dead woman's face; and the servants
Moving; and the icy, hollow noise of the fountain-taps,

Terrible, terrible youth; and the heart empty.
Oh! it will be as it is in this life; the poor voices,
The winter voices in the worn-out suburbs;
And the window-mender's cracked street-cry;

The dirty bonnet, with an old woman under it
Howling a catalogue of stale fish, and the blue-apron'd fellow
Spitting on his chapped hands
And bellowing like an angel of judgement,

It will be exactly as here and in this life, and the table,
The bible, Goethe, the ink with the same temporal odour,
Paper, pale; woman, white thought-reader!
Pen, the portrait.
                    It will be the same,
My child, as in this life, the same garden,
Long, long, tufted, darkish, and, at lunch-time,
Pleasure of being together; that is –
People unacquainted, having only in common
A knowledge of their unacquaintance –

And that one must put on one's best clothes
To go into the night – at the end of things,
Loveless and lampless;
It will be the same as in this life,
The same lane in the forest; and at mid-day, in mid-autumn
When the clean road turns like a weeping woman
To gather the valley flowers,
We will cross in our walks,
    As in the yesterday you have forgotten,
    In the gown whose colour you have forgotten.

Translated by EZRA POUND

Late in the Night

One can't converse with shades
on the phone.
During our mute dialogues there is
no microphone boom or loudspeaker.
However, even words serve
when they don't concern us, picked up
by mistake by a telephone operator
and relayed to someone who
isn't there, doesn't hear.
Once they came from Vancouver
late in the night while I was waiting
for a call from Milan.
At first I was taken aback,
but then hoped that the mix-up would continue.
One voice from the Pacific, the other
from the lagoon. At that time
the two voices talked freely as never
before. Then nothing happened,
we assured the operator that
everything was perfect, in order,
and could continue, in fact *must* continue.
Nor did we ever know who'd foot the bill
for that miracle.
But I didn't remember a single word.
The time zone was different, the other
voice wasn't there, and I
wasn't there for her, even the languages
got mixed up, a hotchpotch of jargons,

curses and laughter. By now
after all these years
the other voice has forgotten and perhaps
thinks I'm dead. I think
it's she who is dead, but was
alive for a second at least,
and did not know it.

Translated by G. SINGH

Beauty Rohtraut

What is the name of King Ringang's daughter?
  Rohtraut, Beauty Rohtraut!
And what does she do the livelong day,
Since she dare not knit and spin alway?
O hunting and fishing is ever her play!
And, heigh! that her huntsman I might be!
I'd hunt and fish right merrily!
    Be silent, heart!

And it chanced that, after this some time, –
  Rohtraut, Beauty Rohtraut, –
The boy in the Castle has gained access,
And a horse he has got and a huntsman's dress,
To hunt and to fish with the merry Princess;
And, O! that a king's son I might be!
Beauty Rohtraut I love so tenderly.
    Hush! hush! my heart.

Under a grey old oak they sat,
  Beauty, Beauty Rohtraut!
She laughs: 'Why look you so slyly at me?
If you have heart enough, come, kiss me.'
Cried the breathless boy, 'Kiss thee?'
But he thinks, kind fortune has favoured my youth;
And thrice he has kissed Beauty Rohtraut's mouth.
    Down! down! mad heart.

Then slowly and silently they rode home, –
    Rohtraut, Beauty Rohtraut!
The boy was lost in his delight:
'And, wert thou Empress this very night,
I would not heed or feel the blight;
Ye thousand leaves of the wild wood wist
How Beauty Rohtraut's mouth I kiss'd.
      Hush! hush! wild heart.'

Translated by GEORGE MEREDITH

Time topples Statyllios like a doddery oak

Time topples Statyllios like a doddery oak.

Death hauls the old queen off, but before he goes,
he solemnly dedicates to the God of Cock:

his summer frocks dyed Dayglo puce
one shoulder-length, blonde, greasy, lacquered wig
two glittering, sequined, high-heeled shoes
an overnight grip stuffed full of drag
and flutes still smelling of cachous and booze.

Translated by TONY HARRISON

Lone Gentleman

Young homosexuals and girls in love,
and widows gone to seed, sleepless, delirious,
and novice housewives pregnant some thirty hours,
the hoarse cats cruising across my garden's shadows
like a necklace of throbbing, sexual oysters
surround my solitary home
like enemies entrenched against my soul,
like conspirators in pyjamas
exchanging long, thick kisses on the sly.

The radiant summer entices lovers here
in melancholic regiments
made up of fat and flabby, gay and mournful couples:
under the graceful palm trees, along the moonlit beach,
there is a continual excitement of trousers and petticoats,
the crisp sound of stockings caressed,
women's breasts shining like eyes.

It's quite clear that the local clerk, bored to the hilt,
after his weekday tedium, cheap paperbacks in bed,
has managed to make his neighbour
and he takes her to the miserable flea-pits
where the heroes are young stallions or passionate princes:
he caresses her legs downy with soft hair
with his wet, hot hands smelling of cigarillos.

Seducer's afternoons and strictly legal nights
fold together like a pair of sheets, burying me:
the siesta hours when young male and female students
as well as priests retire to masturbate,
and when animals screw outright,
and bees smell of blood and furious flies buzz,
and cousins play kinkily with their girl cousins,
and doctors glare angrily at their young patient's husband,
and the professor, almost unconsciously, during the morning
                                                        hours,
copes with his marital duties and then has breakfast,
and, later on, the adulterers who love each other with real love,
on beds as high and spacious as sea-going ships —
so for sure and for ever this great forest surrounds me,
breathing through flowers large as mouths chock full of teeth,
black-rooted in the shapes of hoofs and shoes.

Translated by NATHANIEL TARN

GÉRARD DE NERVAL
1808–1855

The Mute Phenomena

Your great mistake is to disregard the satire
Bandied among the mute phenomena.
Be strong if you must, your brusque hegemony
Means fuck-all to the somnolent sunflower
Or the extinct volcano. What do you know
Of the revolutionary theories advanced
By turnips, or the sex-life of cutlery?
Everything is susceptible, Pythagoras said so.

An ordinary common-or-garden brick wall, the kind
For talking to or banging your head on,
Resents your politics and bad draughtsmanship.
God is alive and lives under a stone.
Already in a lost hub-cap is conceived
The ideal society which will replace our own.

Translated by DEREK MAHON

VITĚZSLAU NEZVAL
1900–1958

The Clock in the Old Jewish Ghetto

While time is running away on Příkopy Street
Like a racing cyclist who thinks he can overtake death's machine
You are like the clock in the ghetto whose hands go backwards
If death surprised me I would die a six-year-old boy

Translated by EWALD OSERS

Elegy 5

In summer's heat and mid-time of the day,
To rest my limbs upon a bed I lay;
One window shut, the other open stood,
Which gave such light, as twinkles in a wood,
Like twilight glimpse at setting of the sun,
Or night being past, and yet not day begun.
Such light to shamefast maidens must be shown,
Where they may sport and seem to be unknown.
Then came Corinna in a long loose gown,
Her white neck hid with tresses hanging down,
Resembling fair Semiramis going to bed,
Or Laïs of a thousand wooers sped.
I snatched her gown; being thin, the harm was small,
Yet strived she to be covered therewithal,
And striving thus as one that would be cast,
Betrayed herself, and yielded at the last.
Stark naked as she stood before mine eye,
Not one wen in her body could I spy.
What arms and shoulders did I touch and see,
How apt her breasts were to be pressed by me!
How smooth a belly under her waist saw I,
How large a leg, and what a lusty thigh!
To leave the rest, all liked me passing well;
I clinged her naked body, down she fell.
Judge you the rest: being tired she bade me kiss;
Jove send me more such afternoons as this.

Translated by CHRISTOPHER MARLOWE

DAN PAGIS
1930–1986

End of the Questionnaire

Housing conditions: number of galaxy and star,
number of grave.
Are you alone or not.
What grass grows on top of you,
and from where (e.g. from your stomach, eyes, mouth, etc.)

You have the right to appeal.

In the blank space below indicate
how long you have been awake and why are you surprised.

Translated by STEPHEN MITCHELL

English Lessons

When it was Desdemona's time to sing,
and so little life was left to her,
she wept, not over love, her star,
but over willow, willow, willow.

When it was Desdemona's time to sing
and her murmuring softened the stones
around the black day, her blacker demon
prepared a psalm of weeping streams.

When it was Ophelia's time to sing,
and so little life was left to her,
the dryness of her soul was swept away
like straws from haystacks in a storm.

When it was Ophelia's time to sing,
and the bitterness of tears was more
than she could bear, what trophies
did she hold? Willow, and columbine.

Stepping out of all that grief,
they entered, with faint hearts
the pool of the universe and quenched
their bodies with other worlds.

Translated by MARK RUDMAN *with* BOHDAN BOYCHUK

In the terrible night, natural substance of all nights

In the terrible night, natural substance of all nights,
In the night of insomnia, natural substance of all my nights,
I remember, awake in tossing drowsiness,
I remember what I've done and what I might have done in life.
I remember, and an anguish
Spreads all through me like a physical chill or a fear,
The irreparable of my past – this is the real corpse.
All the other corpses may very well be illusion.
All the dead may be alive somewhere else,
All my own past moments may be existing somewhere
In the illusion of space and time,
In the falsity of elapsing.

But what I was not, what I did not do, what I did not even dream;
What only now I see I ought to have done,
What only now I clearly see I ought to have been –
This is what is dead beyond all the Gods,
This – and it was, after all, the best of me – is what not even the
                                        Gods bring to life . . .

If at a certain point
I had turned to the left instead of to the right;
If at a certain moment
I had said yes instead of no, or no instead of yes;
If in a certain conversation
I had hit on the phrases which only now, in this half-sleep, I
                                        elaborate –

If all this had been so,
I would be different today, and perhaps the whole universe
Would be insensibly brought to be different as well.

But I did not turn in the direction which is irreparably lost,
Not turn or even think of turning, and only now I perceive it;
But I did not say no or say yes, and only now see what I didn't
say;
But the phrases I failed to say surge up in me at present, all of
them,
Clear, inevitable, natural,
The conversation gathered in conclusively,
The whole matter resolved . . .
But only now what never was, nor indeed shall be, hurts.

What I have missed definitely holds no sort of hope
In any sort of metaphysical system.
Maybe I could bring what I have dreamed to some other world,
But could I bring to another world the things I forgot to dream?
These, yes, the dreams going begging, are the real corpse.
I bury it in my heart for ever, for all time, for all universes,

In this night when I can't sleep and peace encircles me
Like a truth which I've no share in,
And the moonlight outside, like a hope I do not have, is invisible
to me.

Translated by JONATHAN GRIFFIN

Whoso list to hunt, I know where is a hind

Whoso list to hunt, I know where is a hind,
  But as for me, alas, I may no more.
  The vain travail hath wearied me so sore,
  I am of them that farthest comes behind.
Yet may I by no means my wearied mind
  Draw from the Deer, but as she fleeth afore
Fainting I follow. I leave off therefore,
  Since in a net I seek to hold the wind.
Who list her hunt (I put him out of doubt)
  As well as I may spend his time in vain.
  And graven with diamonds in letters plain
There is written her fair neck round about:
  'Noli me tangere, for Caesar's I am,
  And wild for to hold, though I seem tame.'

Translated by SIR THOMAS WYATT

Doing, a filthy pleasure is, and short

Doing, a filthy pleasure is, and short;
And done, we straight repent us of the sport:
Let us not then rush blindly on unto it,
Like lustful beasts, that only know to do it:
For lust will languish, and that heat decay,
But thus, thus, keeping endless Holy-day,
Let us together closely lie, and kiss,
There is no labour, nor no shame in this;
This hath pleased, doth please, and long will please; never
Can this decay, but is beginning ever.

Translated by BEN JONSON

JÁNOS PILINSZKY
1921–1981

On the Back of a Photograph

Hunched I make my way, uncertainly.
The other hand is only three years old.
An eighty-year-old hand and a three-year-old.
We hold each other. We hold each other tight.

Translated by PETER JAY

A Mad Poem Addressed to my Nephews and Nieces

The World cheats those who cannot read;
I, happily, have mastered script and pen.
The World cheats those who hold no office;
I am blessed with high official rank.
Often the old have much sickness and pain;
With me, luckily, there is not much wrong.
People when they are old are often burdened with ties;
But I have finished with marriage and giving in marriage.
No changes happen to jar the quiet of my mind;
No business comes to impair the vigour of my limbs.
Hence it is that now for ten years
Body and soul have rested in hermit peace.
And all the more, in the last lingering years
What I shall need are very few things.
A single rug to warm me through the winter;
One meal to last me the whole day.
It does not matter that my house is rather small;
One cannot sleep in more than one room!
It does not matter that I have not many horses;
One cannot ride on two horses at once!
As fortunate as me among the people of the world
Possibly one would find seven out of ten.
As contented as me among a hundred men
Look as you may, you will not find one.
In the affairs of others even fools are wise;
In their own business even sages err.

To no one else would I dare to speak my heart,
So my wild words are addressed to my nephews and nieces.

Translated by ARTHUR WALEY

He

Some bite off the others'
Arm or leg or whatever

Take it between their teeth
Run off as quick as they can
Bury it in the earth

The others run in all directions
Sniff search sniff search
Turn up all the earth

If any are lucky enough to find their arm
Or leg or whatever
It's their turn to bite

The game goes on briskly

As long as there are arms
As long as there are legs
As long as there is anything whatever

Translated by ANNE PENNINGTON

Pater Noster

Our Father who art in heaven
Stay there
And we'll stay here on earth
Which is sometimes so pretty
With its mysteries of New York
And its mysteries of Paris
At least as good as that of the Trinity
With its little canal at Ourcq
Its great wall of China
Its river at Morlaix
Its candy canes
With its Pacific Ocean
And its two basins in the Tuileries
With its good children and bad people
With all the wonders of the world
Which are here
Simply on the earth
Offered to everyone
Strewn about
Wondering at the wonder of themselves
And daring not avow it
As a naked pretty girl dares not show herself
With the world's outrageous misfortunes
Which are legion
With legionaries
With torturers
With the masters of this world
The masters with their priests their traitors and their troops

With the seasons
With the years
With the pretty girls and with the old bastards
With the straw of misery rotting in the steel
of cannons.

Translated by LAWRENCE FERLINGHETTI

The Prophet

I dragged my steps across a desert bare,
    My spirit parched with heat;
And lo, a seraph with six wings was there;
    He stood where two roads meet.

Soft as the coming of a dream at night,
    His fingers touched my head;
He raised the lids of my prophetic sight,
    An eagle's, wide with dread.

He touched my ears. They filled with sound and song:
    I heard the heaven's motion,
The flight of angels, and the reptile throng
    That moves beneath the ocean.

I heard the soundless growth of plant and tree;
    Then, stooping to my face,
With his right hand he tore my tongue from me,
    Vain, sinful tongue and base.

A serpent's fiery fang he thrust instead
    Through my faint lips apart;
He slit my breast, and with a sword stained red
    Hewed out my quaking heart.

A coal of living fire his fingers placed
    Deep in my gaping side.
Dead as I lay upon the desert waste,
    I heard God's Voice that cried:

'Arise, O prophet, having seen and heard;
Strong in my Spirit, span
The universal earth, and make my word
Burn in the heart of man.'

Translated by FRANCES CORNFORD *and* ESTHER POLIANOWSKY SALAMAN

Antico Inverno

My longing for your waxen hands
clear in the flame's penumbra:
their scent was that of oakwood and of roses
and of death. Winter of the ancients.
It was the birds that, seeking grain,
were suddenly of snow,
likewise our words.
A little sun, a flame of angels,
then the mists; and the trees;
and we compounded of the morning air.

Translated by W. C. FITZGERALD

If you imagine

If you imagine
if you imagine
little sweetie little sweetie
if you imagine
this will this will this
will last forever
this season of
this season of
season of love
you're fooling yourself
little sweetie little sweetie
you're fooling yourself

If you think little one
if you think ah ah
that that rosy complexion
that waspy waist
those lovely muscles
the enamel nails
nymph thigh
and your light foot
if you think little one
that will that will that
will last forever
you're fooling yourself
little sweetie little sweetie
you're fooling yourself

The lovely days disappear
the lovely holidays
suns and planets
go round in a circle
but you my little one
you go straight
toward you know not what
very slowly draw near
the sudden wrinkle
the weighty fat
the triple chin
the flabby muscle
come gather gather
the roses the roses
roses of life
and may their petals
be a calm sea
of happinesses
come gather gather
if you don't do it
you're fooling yourself
little sweetie little sweetie
you're fooling yourself

Translated by MICHAEL BENEDIKT

Time and Again

Time and again, however well we know the landscape of love,
and the little church-yard with lamenting names,
and the frightfully silent ravine wherein all the others
end: time and again we go out two together,
under the old trees, lie down again and again
between the flowers, face to face with the sky.

Translated by J. B. LEISHMAN

ARTHUR RIMBAUD
1854–1891

The Stolen Heart

My sad heart slobbers at the poop,
My heart covered with tobacco-spit:
They spew streams of soup at it,
My sad heart drools at the poop:
Under the jeering of the soldiers
Who break out laughing
My sad heart drools at the poop,
My heart covered with tobacco-spit!

Ithyphallic and soldierish,
Their jeerings have depraved it!
On the rudder you see frescoes
Ithyphallic and soldierish.
O abracadabratic waves,
Take my heart, let it be washed!
Ithyphallic and soldierish,
Their jeerings have depraved it.

When they have used up their quid,
How will I act, O stolen heart?
There will be Bacchic hiccups,
When they have used up their quid:
I will have stomach retchings,
If my heart is degraded:
When they have used up their quid
How will I act, O stolen heart?

Translated by WALLACE FOWLIE

Search

Come in, Gentlemen – he said. No inconvenience. Look through
                                        everything;
I have nothing to hide. Here's the bedroom, here the study,
here the dining-room. Here? – the attic for old things; –
everything wears out, Gentlemen; it's full; everything wears out,
                                        wears out,
so quickly too, Gentlemen; this? – a thimble; – mother's;
this? mother's oil-lamp, mother's umbrella – she loved me
                                        enormously; –
but this forged identity card? this jewellery, somebody else's? the
                                        dirty towel?
this theatre ticket? the shirt with holes? blood stains?
and this photograph? his, yes, wearing a woman's hat covered
                                        with flowers,
inscribed to a stranger – his handwriting –
who planted these in here? who planted these in here? who
                                        planted these in here?

Translated by NIKOS STANGOS

Came to me –

Came to me –
                    Who?

She.

                    When?
In the dawn, afraid.

                    What of?

Anger.
                    Whose?
Her father's.
                    Confide!

I kissed her twice.
                    Where?
On her moist mouth.
                    Mouth?

No.
                    What, then?
Cornelian.
                    How was it?
Sweet.

Translated by BASIL BUNTING

Landscape of Screams

At night when dying proceeds to sever all seams
the landscape of screams
tears open the black bandage,

Above Moria, the falling off cliffs to God,
there hovers the flag of the sacrificial knife
Abraham's scream for the son of his heart,
at the great ear of the Bible it lies preserved.

O hieroglyphs of screams
engraved at the entrance gate to death.

Wounded coral of shattered throat flutes.

O, O hands with finger vines of fear,
dug into wildly rearing manes of sacrificial blood –

Screams, shut tight with the shredded mandibles of fish,
woe tendril of the smallest children
and the gulping train of breath of the very old,

slashed into seared azure with burning tails.
Cells of prisoners, of saints,
tapestried with the nightmare pattern of throats,
seething hell in the doghouse of madness
of shackled leaps –

This is the landscape of screams!
Ascension made of screams
out of the bodies' grate of bones,
arrows of screams, released
from bloody quivers.

Job's scream to the four winds
and the scream concealed in Mount Olive
like a crystal-bound insect overwhelmed by impotence.

O knife of evening red, flung into the throats
where trees of sleep rear blood-licking from the ground,
where time is shed
from the skeletons in Hiroshima and Maidanek.

Ashen scream from visionary eye tortured blind –

O you bleeding eye
in the tattered eclipse of the sun
hung up to be dried by God
in the cosmos –

Translated by MICHAEL ROLOFF

PEDRO SALINAS
1891–1951

Wake up. Day calls you

Wake up. Day calls you
to your life: your duty.
And to live, nothing more.
Root it out of the glum
night and the darkness
that covered your body
for which light waited
on tiptoe in the dawn.
Stand up, affirm the straight
simple will to be
a pure slender virgin.
Test your body's metal.
Cold, heat? Your blood
will tell against the snow,
or behind the window.
The colour
in your cheeks will tell.
And look at people. Rest
doing no more than adding
your perfection to another
day. Your task
is to carry your life high,
and play with it, hurl it
like a voice to the clouds
so it may retrieve the light
already gone from us.

That is your fate: to live.
Do nothing.
Your work is you, nothing more.

Translated by WILLIS BARNSTONE

He is More than a Hero

He is a god in my eyes –
the man who is allowed
to sit beside you – he

who listens intimately
to the sweet murmur of
your voice, the enticing

laughter that makes my own
heart beat fast. If I meet
you suddenly, I can't

speak – my tongue is broken;
a thin flame runs under
my skin; seeing nothing,

hearing only my own ears
drumming, I drip with sweat;
trembling shakes my body

and I turn paler than
dry grass. At such times
death isn't far from me

Translated by MARY BARNARD

VICTOR SEGALEN
1878–1919

Mongol Libation

It's here we took him alive. As he fought well we offered him some office: he preferred to serve his Prince in death.

We cut his hamstrings: he waved his arms about to witness to his zeal. We cut his arms: he bellowed his devotion to Him.

We sliced his mouth from ear to ear: he signalled with his eyes that he remained faithful.

Let's not pierce his eyes as one does to cowards. Let's cut his head off respectfully, and pour the *koumys* of the brave, with this libation:

When you are reborn, Cheng-ho-chang, do us the honour of being reborn among us.

Translated by NATHANIEL TARN

Hell

Oh the magnificence of hell!
In hell no one speaks of death.
Hell is walled up in the bowels of the earth
and adorned with glowing flowers . . .
In hell no one says an empty word . . .
In hell no one has drunk and no one has slept
and no one rests and no one sits still.
In hell no one speaks but everyone screams,
there, tears are not tears and all grief is powerless.
In hell no one falls ill and no one tires.
Hell is constant and eternal.

Translated by STINA KATCHADOURIAN

All the planets in heaven, all the stars

All the planets in heaven, all the stars,
gave my lord their graces at his conception;
all gave him their special gifts,
to make one perfect mortal man.
Saturn gave loftiness of understanding,
Jove the desire for noble deeds,
Mars more skill in war than any other,
Phoebus Apollo elegance and wit.
Venus gave him beauty and gentle ways,
Mercury eloquence; but the moon alone
made him too freezing cold for me.
Every one of these rare graces
makes me burn for his brilliant flame,
and one alone has turned him into ice.

Translated by SALLY PURCELL

Rain and the Tyrants

I stand and watch the rain
Falling in pools which make
Our grave old planet shine;
The clear rain falling, just the same
As that which fell in Homer's time
And that which dropped in Villon's day
Falling on mother and on child
As on the passive backs of sheep;
Rain saying all it has to say
Again and yet again, and yet
Without the power to make less hard
The wooden heads of tyrants or
To soften their stone hearts,
And powerless to make them feel
Amazement as they ought;
A drizzling rain which falls
Across all Europe's map,
Wrapping all men alive
In the same moist envelope;
Despite the soldiers loading arms,
Despite the newspapers' alarms,
Despite all this, all that,
A shower of drizzling rain
Making the flags hang wet.

Translated by DAVID GASCOYNE

LADY SUTE-JO
1633–1698

Woman

Woman –
how hot the skin
she covers.

Translated by LUCIEN STRYK *and* TAKASHI IKEMOTO

I dreamed this dream and I still dream of it

I dreamed this dream and I still dream of it
and I will dream of it sometime again.
Everything repeats itself and everything will be reincarnated,
and my dreams will be your dreams.

There, to one side of us, to one side of the world
wave after wave breaks on the shore:
there's a star on the wave, and a man, and a bird,
reality and dreams and death – wave after wave.

Dates are irrelevant. I was, I am, I will be.
Life is a miracle of miracles, and I kneel
before the miracle alone like an orphan,

alone in the mirrors, enclosed in reflections,
seas and towns, shining brightly through the smoke.
A mother cries and takes her baby on her knee.

Translated by RICHARD MCKANE

The Death of Adonis

When Venus her Adonis found,
Just slain, and weltering on the ground,
With hair disordered, ghastly look,
And cheeks their roses had forsook;
She bade the Cupids fetch with speed,
The Boar that did this horrid deed:
They, to revenge Adonis blood,
As quick as birds searched all the wood,
And straight the murderous creature found,
Whom they, with chains, securely bound;
And whilst his net one o'er him flung,
To drag the captive Boar along
Another followed with his bow,
Pushing to make him faster go;
Who most unwillingly obeyed,
For he of Venus was afraid.
   No sooner she the Boar espied,
But, Oh! Thou cruel Beast, she cried,
That hadst the heart to wound this thigh,
How couldst thou kill so sweet a boy?
   Great Goddess (said the Boar, and stood
Trembling) I swear by all that's good,
By thy fair self, by Him I've slain,
These pretty hunters, and this chain;
I did no harm this youth intend,
Much less had thought to kill your friend:
I gazed, and with my passion strove,
For with his charms I fell in love:

At last that naked thigh of his,
With lovers heat I ran to kiss;
Oh fatal cause of all my woe!
'Twas then I gave the heedless blow.
These tusks with utmost rigour draw,
Cut, break, or tear them from my jaw,
'Tis just I should these teeth remove,
Teeth that can have a sense of love;
Or this revenge, if yet too small,
Cut off the kissing lips and all.

  When Venus heard this humble tale,
Pity did o'er her rage prevail,
She bade them straight his chains untie,
And set the Boar at liberty;
Who never to wood returned again,
But followed Venus in her train,
And when by chance to fire he came,
His amorous tusks singed in the flame.

Translated by PHILIP AYRES

Summer

At evening, the sound of the cuckoo
Stops in the wood.
The grain bends lower,
The red poppy.

Black thunderclouds bloom
Above the hill.
The ancient song of the cricket
Fades off into the fields.

The leaves of the chestnut
Tree stir no more.
Upon the spiral staircase
Your dress rustles.

One silent candle shines
In the dark room;
A silvery hand
Extinguishes it;

No wind, no stars. Night.

Translated by ROBERT GENIER

I know the truth – give up all other truths!

I know the truth – give up all other truths!
No need for people anywhere on earth to struggle.
Look – it is evening, look, it is nearly night:
what do you speak of, poets, lovers, generals?

The wind is level now, the earth is wet with dew,
the storm of stars in the sky will turn to quiet.
And soon all of us will sleep under the earth, we
who never let each other sleep above it.

Translated by ELAINE FEINSTEIN

Easing My Heart

By river and lakes at odds with life I journeyed, wine my freight:
Slim waists of Ch'u broke my heart, light bodies danced into my
                                                            palm.
Ten years late I wake at last out of my Yang-chou dream
With nothing but the name of a drifter in the blue houses.

Translated by A. C. GRAHAM

'Blue houses': brothels.

Way

what is this road that separates us
across which I hold out the hand of my thoughts
a flower is written at the end of each finger
and the end of the road is a flower which walks with you

Translated by LEE HARWOOD

Christmas

I have no wish
to plunge
into a web
of streets

On my shoulders
I feel
such weariness

Leave me like this
like a
thing
laid down
in a
corner
and forgotten

Here
one feels
nothing
but the good warmth

I stay
with the four
caprioles
of smoke
from the stove

Naples, December 26th 1916

Translated by MICHAEL HAMBURGER

CÉSAR VALLEJO
1892–1938

Black Stone on Top of a White Stone

I shall die in Paris, in a rainstorm,
On a day I already remember.
I shall die in Paris – it does not bother me –
Doubtless on a Thursday, like today, in autumn.

It shall be a Thursday, because today, Thursday
As I put down these lines, I have set my shoulders
To the evil. Never like today have I turned,
And headed my whole journey to the ways where I am alone.

César Vallejo is dead. They struck him,
All of them, though he did nothing to them.
They hit him hard with a stick and hard also
With the end of a rope. Witnesses are: the Thursdays,
The shoulder bones, the loneliness, the rain and the roads . . .

Translated by THOMAS MERTON

In that café crowded with fools we stood

In that café crowded with fools we stood
(Just us two) for the hideous turpitude
Of liking men: they never thought, the cunts,
We shat on their dim-witted innocence,
Their standard loves, their tinny golden rules
While holding to our principles and tools
We swung and parried to our hearts' content,
Veiled in a cloud our peaceful pipes had sent –
Like Zeus and Hera in their nebulous bed –
Till our two Punch's noses, glad and red,
Wiped by our fingers with delightful squeezes
Under the table jetted great white sneezes.

Translated by ALISTAIR ELLIOT

FRANÇOIS VILLON
1431–?

The Ballad of Dead Ladies

Tell me now in what hidden way is
　　Lady Flora the lovely Roman?
Where's Hipparchia, and where is Thais,
　　Neither of them the fairer woman?
　　Where is Echo, beheld of no man,
Only heard on river and mere, –
　　She whose beauty was more than human? . . .
But where are the snows of yester-year?

Where's Heloise, the learned nun,
　　For whose sake Abeillard, I ween,
Lost manhood and put priesthood on?
　　(From Love he won such dule and teen!)
　　And where, I pray you, is the Queen
Who willed that Buridan should steer
　　Sewed in a sack's mouth down the Seine? . . .
But where are the snows of yester-year?

White Queen Blanche, like a queen of lilies,
　　With a voice like any mermaiden –
Bertha Broadfoot, Beatrice, Alice,
　　And Ermengarde the lady of Maine, –
　　And that good Joan whom Englishmen
At Rouen doomed and burned her there, –
　　Mother of God, where are they then? . . .
But where are the snows of yester-year?

131

Nay, never ask this week, fair lord,
    Where they are gone, nor yet this year,
Except with this for an overword, –
    But where are the snows of yester-year?

Translated by DANTE GABRIEL ROSSETTI

Copa: The Barmaid

O Syrian dancing-girl with the filleted hair,
who taught you to swing your flanks with that shiver and shake?
She's dancing drunk in the tavern's smoky air,
lewd wench, to the clicketing sound the castanets make.

Why stay in the dusty heat where everything withers?
Come here, lie down, and be drunk awhile, you fool.
Look! tankards, cups, bowls, roses, flutes, and zithers,
and a trellis-arbor shadowed by reeds and cool.

In a cave full of music, like Pan's own cave, you can stretch –
the kind of piping you hear 'neath the open sky.
Thin wine just drawn from a pitchy cask they'll fetch,
and, brabbling and murmuring, water goes swiftly by.

Look! there are wreaths from crocus and violets wrought,
gold melilot mixed with the rose's crimson hue.
From the virgin stream of Acheloïs are brought
lilies in willow-baskets – and all for you.

Look! little cheeses drying in baskets of rush,
and plums that come to their sweetness in autumn weather;
chestnuts, and apples with red that is pleasantly lush.
Look! fine Ceres and Love and Bacchus together.

Look! reddened blackberries, grapes in placid clusters,
sea-green cucumbers hanging from tendrils of shade.
Look! the arbor-god – with his willow-hook he blusters,
but even his terrible middle won't make us afraid.

Hither O wanderer. The little ass sweats, and he faints.
The dear little ass is Vesta's own darling. So spare.
The crickets are splitting the thickets with shrilling complaints,
The lizard is lurking cool in a bramble-lair.

Be wise and drench out the heat with wine in a glass
Or a crystal cup, if that's how you like your wine.
Lie tired in the vine-shade and let the summer hours pass,
And round your nodding head let the roses twine.

Yes, reap the kisses from someone mouth-open, kindly.
Death to the fellows whose questioning eyebrows frowned!
Why keep your wreaths for the ashes huddled blindly?
See your life and not your tombstone with roses crowned.

To hell with the future! Bring wine and the dice-box here.
'I'm coming, so kiss,' says Death, and pinches my ear.

Translated by JACK LINDSAY

The Celestial Fire

Now an angel of the Lord appeared to
Moses in a blazing fire –

a fire that devours fire; a fire that burns
in things dry and moist; a fire that
glows amid snow and ice; a fire that is
like a crouching lion; a fire that reveals
itself in many forms; a fire that is, and
never expires; a fire that shines and
roars; a fire that blazes and sparkles; a
fire that flies in a storm wind; a fire
that burns without wood; a fire that
renews itself every day; a fire that is
not fanned by fire; a fire that billows
like palm branches; a fire whose sparks
are flashes of lightning; a fire black as
a raven; a fire, curled, like the colours
of the rainbow!

Translated by T. CARMI

An Elegy

I

O youngest, best-loved daughter of Hsieh,
Who unluckily married this penniless scholar,
You patched my clothes from your own wicker basket,
And I coaxed off your hairpins of gold, to buy wine with;
For dinner we had to pick wild herbs –
And to use dry locust-leaves for our kindling.
. . . Today they are paying me a hundred thousand –
And all that I can bring to you is a temple-sacrifice.

II

We joked, long ago, about one of us dying,
But suddenly, before my eyes, you are gone.
Almost all your clothes have been given away;
Your needlework is sealed, I dare not look at it . . .
I continue your bounty to our men and our maids –
Sometimes, in a dream, I bring you gifts.
. . . This is a sorrow that all mankind must know –
But not as those know it who have been poor together.

III

I sit here alone, mourning for us both.
How many years do I lack now of my threescore and ten?
There have been better men than I to whom heaven denied a son,
There was a poet better than I whose dead wife could not hear
him.

What have I to hope for in the darkness of our tomb?
You and I had little faith in a meeting after death –
Yet my open eyes can see all night
That lifelong trouble of your brow.

Translated by WITTER BYNNER

Chronological List of Poets

Sappho	7th century BC	Greek
Anacreontea	6th century BC	Greek
Amergin	5th century BC	Irish
Anonymous (Psalm 137)	5th century BC	Hebrew
Antiphanes	4th century BC	Greek
Theocritus	c. 308–240 BC	Greek
Anonymous (Song of Songs: 7)	3rd or 2nd century BC	Hebrew
Myrinos	c. 90 BC–AD 50	Greek
Catullus	c. 84–c. 54 BC	Roman
Virgil	70–19 BC	Roman
Horace	65–8 BC	Roman
Ovid	43 BC–AD 18	Roman
Petronius Arbiter	d. AD 66	Roman
Martial	AD 40–104	Roman
Yannai	?6th century	Hebrew
Anonymous (The King of Connacht)	600–1200	Irish
Li Po	701–762	Chinese
Po Chu-I	772–846	Chinese
Yüan Chên	799–831	Chinese
Lady Ki no Washika	8th century	Japanese
Tu Mu	803–852	Chinese
Rudaki	?870–940/41	Persian
Samuel Hanagid	993–1056	Hebrew
Bernart de Ventadorn	fl. c. 1145–1180	French
Judah Al-Harizi	c. 1170–after 1235	Hebrew
Isobel Campbell	c. 1200	Irish
Jacopone da Todi	1228–1306	Italian
Dante Alighieri	1265–1321	Italian
Francesco Petrarch	1304–1374	Italian
Dafydd Ap Gwilym	fl. 1340–1370	Welsh
François Villon	1431–?	French
Michelangelo Buonarroti	1475–1564	Italian
Joachim du Bellay	1522–1560	French
Gaspara Stampa	c. 1523–1554	Italian
Lady Sute-Jo	1633–1698	Japanese
Sor Juana Inés de la Cruz	1652–1695	Mexican
Heinrich Heine	1797–1856	German

Giacomo Leopardi	1798–1837	Italian
Aleksandr Pushkin	1799–1837	Russian
American Indian	19th century	American Indian
Eduard Mörike	1804–1875	German
Gérard de Nerval	1808–1855	French
Mikhail Lermontov	1814–1841	Russian
Charles Baudelaire	1821–1867	French
Stéphane Mallarmé	1842–1898	French
Paul Verlaine	1844–1896	French
Arthur Rimbaud	1854–1891	French
Innokenty Annensky	1856–1909	Russian
Jules Laforgue	1860–1887	French
C. P. Cavafy	1863–1933	Greek
Antonio Machado	1875–1939	Spanish
Rainer Maria Rilke	1875–1926	Austrian
O. V. de L. Milosz	1877–1939	Lithuanian/French
Victor Segalen	1878–1919	French
Guillaume Apollinaire	1880–1918	French
Aleksandr Blok	1880–1921	Russian
Valéry Larbaud	1881–1957	French
Juan Ramón Jiménez	1881–1958	Spanish
Jules Supervielle	1884–1960	French
Velimir Khlebnikov	1885–1922	Russian
Pierre Jean Jouve	1887–1976	French
Blaise Cendrars	1887–1961	Swiss
Georg Trakl	1887–1914	Austrian
Fernando Pessoa	1888–1935	Portuguese
Giuseppe Ungaretti	1888–1970	Italian
Anna Akhmatova	1889–1966	Russian
Boris Pasternak	1890–1960	Russian
Pedro Salinas	1891–1951	Spanish
Osip Mandelstam	1891–1938	Russian
Nelly Sachs	1891–1970	German
Edith Södergran	1892–1923	Swedish–Finnish
Marina Tsvetayeva	1892–1941	Russian
César Vallejo	1892–1938	Peruvian
Vladimir Mayakovsky	1893–1930	Russian
Paul Éluard	1895–1952	French
Kaneko Mitsuharu	1895–1975	Japanese
Eugenio Montale	1896–1981	Italian
Tristan Tzara	1896–1963	Romanian
André Breton	1896–1966	French
Louis Aragon	1897–1982	French
Bertolt Brecht	1898–1956	German
Federico García Lorca	1898–1936	Spanish
Henri Michaux	1899–1984	Belgian
Vitězslau Nezval	1900–1958	Czech

Jacques Prévert	1900–1977	French
Salvatore Quasimodo	1901–1968	Italian
Carlos Drummond de Andrade	1902–1987	Brazilian
Nazim Hikmet	1902–1963	Turkish
Raymond Queneau	1903–1976	French
Pablo Neruda	1904–1973	Chilean
Attila József	1905–1937	Hungarian
Arseny Tarkovsky	1907–1989	Russian
Yánnis Rítsos	1909–1990	Greek
Primo Levi	1919–1987	Italian
Paul Celan	1920–1970	German
Erich Fried	1921–1988	Austrian
János Pilinszky	1921–1981	Hungarian
Vasko Popa	1922–1991	Yugoslavian
Dan Pagis	1930–1986	former USSR/Israeli

Index of Translators

Index of First Lines

Acknowledgements

For permission to reprint copyright material the publishers gratefully acknowledge the following:

ANNA AKHMATOVA: 'I am not among those who left our land' from *Selected Poems* (Bloodaxe, 1989) translated by Richard McKane, reprinted by permission of Bloodaxe Books.

AMERGIN: 'Amergin's Charm' from *The Alphabet Calendar of Amergin* by Robert Graves, by permission of A.P. Watt Ltd on behalf of The Trustees of the Robert Graves Copyright Trust.

INNOKENTY ANNENSKY: 'Black Spring' from *Imitations* by Robert Lowell (Faber, 1962). Copyright © 1961 by Robert Lowell. Copyright renewed © 1989 by Caroline Lowell, Harriet Lowell and Sheridan Lowell. Reprinted by permission of Farrar, Straus & Giroux, Inc. and Faber and Faber Limited.

ANONYMOUS: 'The King of Connacht' from *The Penguin Book of Irish Verse* edited by Brendan Kennelly (Penguin Books, 1987), reprinted by permission of the Peters Fraser & Dunlop Group Ltd.

ANTIPHANES: 'Piddle-paddling race of critics, rhizome-fanciers' from *The Greek Anthology* edited by Peter Jay (Penguin, 1981), by permission of Edwin Morgan.

LOUIS ARAGON: 'The Lilacs and the Roses' from *The Collected Poems of Louis MacNeice* edited by E.R. Dodds (Faber, 1966), by permission of Faber and Faber Limited.

BERNART DE VENTADORN: 'The Lark' from *The Translations of Ezra Pound* (Faber, 1963), by permission of Faber and Faber Limited and New Directions.

BERTOLT BRECHT: 'War Has Been Given a Bad Name' from *Poems 1913–1956* translated by J. Willett (Methuen 1976), by permission of Reed International Books.

ISOBEL CAMPBELL: 'A Learned Mistress' from *Kings, Lords and Commons* (Macmillan), by permission of Peters Fraser & Dunlop Group Ltd.

CATULLUS: 'Less pub than brothel, and you, the regulars' from *In the Trojan Ditch* by C.H. Sisson (Carcanet, 1974), by permission of Carcanet Press Limited.

C.P. CAVAFY: 'The City' from *Collected Poems of C.P. Cavafy* translated by Rae Dalven (Hogarth Press, 1971), by permission of Random Century Group.

PAUL CELAN: 'Deathfugue' from *The Poetry of Survival* edited by Daniel Weissbort (Anvil Press, 1992), by permission of John Felstiner.

PAUL ÉLUARD: 'The Invention' translated by Samuel Beckett, by permission of The Samuel Beckett Estate.

ERICH FRIED: 'The Measures Taken' from *German Poetry 1910–1975* (Carcanet Press, 1977), by permission of Michael Hamburger.

SAMUEL HANAGID: 'The Prison' from *The Penguin Book of Hebrew Verse* translated by T. Carmi (Allen Lane, 1981), copyright © T. Carmi, 1981.

NAZIM HIKMET: 'A Sad State of Freedom' from *A Sad State of Freedom* (Greville Press, 1990), by permission of Greville Press.

JACOPONE DA TODI: 'The Stabat Mater' from George Barker, *Collected Poems* (Faber, 1987), by permission of Faber and Faber Limited.

ATTILA JÓZSEF: 'The Seventh' by permission of Carcanet Press.

SOR JUANA INES DE LA CRUZ: 'This coloured conterfeit that thou beholdest' translated by Samuel Beckett, by permission of The Samuel Beckett Estate.

KANEKO MITSUHARU: 'Opposition' from *The Penguin Book of Japanese Verse* translated by Geoffrey Bownas and Anthony Thwaite (Penguin Books, 1964), copyright © Geoffrey Bownas and Anthony Thwaite, 1964, by permission of Penguin Books Limited.

VELIMIR KHLEBNIKOV: 'We chant and enchant' from *The King of Time* (Harvard University Press, 1985), reprinted by permission of Harvard University Press, copyright © 1985 by the Dia Art Foundation.

JULES LAFORGUE: 'For the Book of Love' translated by Vernon Watkins, by permission of Gwen Watkins.

GIACOMO LEOPARDI: 'To Himself' from John Heath-Stubbs, *Collected Poems* (Carcanet, 1988), by permission of David Higham Associates.

MIKHAIL LERMONTOV: 'The Testament' from *Poems from the Russian* edited by Frances Cornford and Esther Polianowsky Salaman (Faber, 1943), by permission of Faber and Faber Limited.

PRIMO LEVI: 'Shemà' from Primo Levi, *Collected Poems* translated by Ruth Feldman and Brian Swann (Faber, 1988), by permission of Faber and Faber Limited.

LI PO: 'The River Merchant's Wife: A Letter' from *Collected Shorter Poems of Ezra Pound* (Faber, 1949), by permission of Faber and Faber Limited and New Directions Publishing Corporation.

FEDERICO GARCÍA LORCA: 'The Faithless Wife' from *Selected Poems* (Penguin, 1960), by permission of The Estate of Federico García Lorca.

ANTONIO MACHADO: 'The Ephemeral Past' from Charles Tomlinson, *Selected Poems 1951–1974* (OUP, 1978), © Charles Tomlinson 1978. Reprinted by permission of Oxford University Press.

STÉPHANE MALLARMÉ: 'A lace curtain self-destructs', by permission of Christopher Reid.

OSIP MANDELSTAM: 'The Stalin Epigram' from *Selected Poems* translated by Clarence Brown and W.S. Merwin (OUP, 1973), reprinted by permission of Oxford University Press.

149